# The Gifts

## Kasia Reay

### Illustrated by Alette Straathof

Schofield & Sims

At w<u>ee</u>kends, F<u>ait</u>h and Abig<u>ai</u>l went to the m<u>ar</u>ket wi<u>th</u> Elizabe<u>th</u>. They were her little help<u>er</u>s.

"There are lots of vitamins in fresh food," Elizabeth said. "It is so good for us."

"Do you need peppers, Elizabeth?
Or some yams?" said Faith.

"Shall we get some plump plums and some sweet corn?" said Abigail.

When Elizabeth had to rest her legs, they sat down and had some roast nuts.

When she was having a long chat, Faith and Abigail had fun looking at all the bright cloth.

One weekend, Elizabeth got sick, so Faith and Abigail did all the shopping for her.

"We got you green peppers, yams and corn," said Faith. "You need the good vitamins, Elizabeth!" said Abigail.

Soon Elizabeth was much better.
"The vitamins did the trick!" she said.

"I have some gifts to thank you for helping me," she said.

"Do you like them?" Elizabeth said. "Now my little helpers look as bright as peppers and as sweet as corn!"